GW01071891

This Book Belongs To

_____

THE WEDDING BOOK

A Bride's Memento

Ariel Books

Andrews and McMeel

Kansas City

10 9 8 7 6 5

ISBN: 0-8362-3011-6

Library of Congress Catalog Card Number: 91-77098

Marbleized endpapers © 1985 by Katherine Radcliffe

Design by Maura Fadden Rosenthal

Introduction

From the proposal to the wedding night, each moment in the nuptial ritual presents a treasured memory to any young bride. It is the very focus of the woman's hopes and dreams, and the launching point to her future marriage.

Gathered here are wedding traditions and customs; touching and amusing lore handed down from generation to generation; and suggestions for readings that will express the profound love between bride and groom. This book contains all the information a young bride needs as she stands at the portals of wedded life—that magical and mysterious union of two loving souls . . .

The wedding.

THE PROPOSAL

Marriage: that I call the will of two to create the one who is more than those who created it.

Friedrich Nietzsche

Miranda: I am your wife, if you will marry
 me;
If not I'll die your maid: to be your fellow
You may deny me; but I'll be your servant
Whether you will or no.
Ferdinand: My mistress, dearest;
And thus I humble ever.
Miranda: My husband then?
Ferdinand: Ay, with a heart as willing
As bondage e'er of freedom; here's my hand.
Miranda: And mine, with my heart in't.

William Shakespeare,

THE TEMPEST

So ancient is the desire of one another which is implanted in us, reuniting our original nature, seeking to make one of two, and to heal the state of man. Each of us when separated, having one side only, like a flat fish, is but the tally-half of a man, and he is always looking for his other half.

Plato

Two Victorian Proposals

He entered. He stood before me. What his words were you can imagine; his manner you can hardly realise, nor can I forget it. He made me, for the first time, feel what it costs a man to declare affection when he doubts response. . . .

Charlotte Brontë,

remembering her husband's proposal

I go about murmuring, 'I have made that dignified girl commit herself, I have, I have,' and then I vault over the sofa with exultation.

Walter Bagehot,

in a letter to his betrothed

Some Thoughts on
Marriage Proposals

It is always incomprehensible to a man that a woman should ever refuse an offer of marriage.

Jane Austen

For talk six times with the same single lady,
And you may get the wedding dress ready.

George Gordon, Lord Byron

*My most brilliant achievement was to be able
to persuade my wife to marry me.*

                                    Winston Churchill

Love is being stupid together.

                                    Paul Valéry

Some people fall in love with the swiftness and force of an electric shock, while with others the process is so gradual that the fact is not discovered until some accident or emergency reveals it to the interior perception.

Jennie June

TALKS ON WOMEN'S TOPICS

1864

Marriage must exemplify friendship's highest ideal, or else it will be a failure.

Margaret E. Sangster

Some young ladies think it smart to encourage a proposal and then refuse it. This is not a sign of good breeding; besides, her motives will soon become generally known, and she will be regarded as a "flirt."

A. E. Davis

AMERICAN ETIQUETTE AND
RULES OF POLITENESS

1882

But granting that a young man and a young woman love one another, have health, have courage and honor, they need not be deterred from marrying because they have little money. The very smallest income that may be depended upon will do as a beginning.

Margaret E. Sangster

Engagement Rings

In medieval times, engagement rings were symbols of a suitor's honorable intentions and served as partial payment for the right to court a bride.

The "gimmal ring," created in the sixteenth century, came out of the engagement ring tradition. A gimmal ring was set with three interlocking rings. The groom, bride, and a family friend or witness each wore one part of the ring until the wedding day. At the wedding ceremony, the three rings were united as one and given to the bride to wear.

The tradition of using precious stones on engagement rings began in the nineteenth century. Although many brides choose diamonds for their engagement rings, it's also popular to select another stone to symbolize the devotion of one's intended.

For the Bride Who Chooses a Birthstone for Her Engagement Ring

January ⁓ Garnet, symbol of constancy and fidelity

February ⁓ Amethyst, symbol of power

March ⁓ Bloodstone, symbol of bravery and wisdom

April ⁓ Diamond, symbol of purity and innocence

May ⁓ Emerald, symbol of loyalty and friendship

June ⁓ Pearl, symbol of good health and beauty

July ✢ Ruby, symbol of nobility and courage

August ✢ Sardonyx, symbol of marital happiness

September ✢ Sapphire, symbol of truth and sincerity

October ✢ Opal, symbol of fearlessness and consistency

November ✢ Topaz, symbol of strength and cheerfulness

December ✢ Turquoise, symbol of prosperity and success

A Final Thought

The best way to hold a man is in your arms.

Mae West

THE CEREMONY

The Man shall answer,
I will.

Selecting the day for the wedding is traditionally the bride's decision. The following are old folk sayings to help brides pick the big day.

Selecting a Month

Marry when the year is new,
Always loving, kind, and true.

When February birds do mate
You may wed, nor dread your fate.

If you wed when March winds blow,
Joy and sorrow both you'll know.

Marry in April when you can,
Joy for maiden and for man.

Marry in the month of May,
You will surely rue the day.

Marry when June roses blow,
Over land and sea you'll go.

They who in July do wed
Must labor always for their bread.

Whoever wed in August be,
Many a change are sure to see.

Marry in September's shine,
Your living will be rich and fine.

If in October you do marry,
Love will come, but riches tarry.

If you wed in bleak November
Only joy will come, remember.

When December's snows fall fast,
Marry, and true love will last.

Selecting the Day of the Week

Monday for health,
Tuesday for wealth,
Wednesday the best day of all;
Thursday for losses,
Friday for crosses,
And Saturday no luck at all.

The Wedding Dress

It has been traditional since the mid-eighteenth century for a bride to wear white. This verse, from a book on etiquette published in 1907, relates traditions on wearing other colors on one's wedding day.

Married in gray, you will go far away.

Married in black, you will wish yourself back.

Married in brown, you will live out of town.

Married in red, you will wish yourself dead.

Married in pearl, you will live in a whirl.

Married in green, ashamed to be seen.

Married in yellow, ashamed of your fellow.

Married in blue, he will always be true.

Married in pink, your spirits will sink.

Married in white, you have chosen aright.

Here is a familiar rhyme:

Something old,
something new,
something borrowed,
something blue.

This tradition is age-old. It is usually interpreted this way:

Something old is the garter of a happily married woman.

Something new is the wedding dress.

Something borrowed is a gold coin, which represents the sun. (Many people believed that the coin should be borrowed from the groom, and worn in the bride's shoe during the ceremony.)

Something blue represents the moon. In the ancient world the goddess of the moon, Diana, was the traditional protector of women.

The wedding veil is a traditional part of the wedding costume. Its original purpose was to keep the "evil eye" of a jealous suitor from seeing the bride and ruining the marriage.

Wedding Flowers

Here are ten plants often used at weddings:

Honeysuckle ∽ Long a symbol of faithful love.

Ivy ∽ A symbol of fidelity, ivy wreaths were worn by brides and grooms in ancient Greece.

Lily ∽ Roman brides and grooms were crowned with lilies, a symbol of purity associated with Juno, goddess of marriage.

Lily of the Valley ∽ This flower is believed to encourage virtue and faithfulness.

Marjoram ∽ Ancient Greek and Roman couples wore crowns of wild marjoram.

Myrtle ∽ Many German brides wear myrtle wreaths, symbol of love and constancy.

Rose ∽ Symbol of love.

Rosemary ∽ An emblem of fidelity, rosemary sprigs often were given as favors at weddings in the past, and a few leaves were often mixed into the wedding cake.

Rue — Sometimes woven (together with rosemary, rowan berries, and flowers) into a wedding wreath by the bride on her wedding eve; the Polish expression "sow rue" meant to be marriageable.

Yarrow — According to tradition, when a wedding couple carries this plant, they will enjoy at least seven years of married bliss.

Readings for a Wedding Ceremony

Sonnet XVIII

Shall I compare thee to a Summer's day?
Thou art more lovely and more temperate:
Rough windes do shake the darling buds of
    Maie,
And Summer's lease hath all too short a
    date:
Sometimes too hot the eye of heaven shines,
And often is his gold complexion dimm'd,
And every faire from faire some-time de-
    clines,

By chance, or nature's changing course un-
   trimm'd:
But thy eternall Summer shall not fade,
Nor lose possession of that faire thou ow'st,
Nor shall death brag thou wandr'st in his
   shade,
When in eternall lines to time thou grow'st,
So long as men can breathe or eyes can see,
So long lives this, and this gives life to thee.

                              William Shakespeare

Sonnet CXVI

Let me not to the marriage of true minds
Admit impediments. Love is not love
Which alters when it alteration finds,
Or bends with the remover to remove.
O no! it is an ever-fixed mark,
That looks on tempests and is never shaken;
It is the star to every wand'ring bark,

Whose worth's unknown, although his height
    be taken.
Love's not Time's fool, though rosy lips and
    cheeks
Within his bending sickle's compass come,
Love alters not with his brief hours and
    weeks,
But bears it out even to the edge of doom:
If this be error and upon me proved,
I never writ, nor no man ever loved.

William Shakespeare

The Passionate Shepherd
To His Love

Come live with me and be my love,
And we will all the pleasures prove
That valleys, groves, hills, and fields,
Woods, or steepy mountain yields.

And we will sit upon the rocks,
Seeing the shepherds feed their flocks,
By shallow rivers to whose falls
Melodious birds sing madrigals.

And I will make thee beds of roses
And a thousand fragrant posies,
A cap of flowers, and a kirtle
Embroidered all with leaves of myrtle;

A gown made of the finest wool
Which from our pretty lambs we pull;
Fair lined slippers for the cold,
With buckles of the purest gold;

A belt of straw and ivy buds,
With coral clasps and amber studs:
And if these pleasures may thee move,
Come live with me, and be my love.

The shepherd's swains shall dance and sing
For thy delight each May morning:
If these delights thy mind may move,
Then live with me and be my love.

Christopher Marlowe

Fulfillment

There is no happier life
But in a wife;
The comforts are so sweet
When two do meet.
'Tis plenty, peace, a calm
Like dropping balm;
Love's weather is so fair,
Like perfumed air.
Each word such pleasure brings
Like soft-touched strings;
Love's passion moves the heart
On either part;

Such harmony together,
So pleased in either.
No discords; concords still;
Sealed with one will.
By love, God made man one,
Yet not alone.
Like stamps of king and queen
It may be seen:
Two figures on one coin,
So do they join,
Only they not embrace.
We, face to face.

William Cavendish

I love thee with a love I seemed to lose

With my lost saints—I love thee with the
breath,

Smiles, tears, of all my life!—and, if God
choose,

I shall but love thee better after death.

Elizabeth Barrett Browning

Nought beneath the sky
More sweet, more worthy is, than firm con-
  sent
Of man and wife in household government.
It joys their wishers-well, their enemies
  wounds
But to themselves the special good redounds.

       Homer (Trans. George Chapman)

Romance

I will make you brooches and toys for your
    delight
Of birdsong at morning and starshine at night
I will make a palace fit for you and me
Of green days in forests and blue days at sea.

I will make my kitchen and you shall keep
    your room
Where white flows the river and bright blows
    the broom,
And you shall wash your linen and keep your
    body white
In rainfall at morning and dewfall at night.

And this shall be for music when no one else
    is near,
The fine song for singing, the rare song to
    hear!
That only I remember, that only you admire,
Of the broad road that stretches and the
    roadside fire.

                            Robert Louis Stevenson

Two Scriptural Readings for a Wedding

From the very first [God] made man and woman to be joined together permanently in marriage; therefore a man is to leave his father and mother, and he and his wife are united so that they are no longer two, but one. And no man may separate what God has joined together.

Mark 10:6-9

Love is patient and kind; love is not jealous or boastful; it is not arrogant or rude. Love does not insist on its own way; it is not irritable or resentful; it does not rejoice at wrong, but rejoices in the right. Love bears all things, believes all things, hopes all things, endures all things. Love never ends; . . . So faith, hope, love abide, these three; but the greatest of these is love.

I Corinthians 13:4-8, 13

The Symbolism of the
Wedding Ring

"The wedding-ring, symbolical of the conjugal relation, has ever been the accepted accompaniment of marriage. Its being put on the fourth finger of the left hand has been continued, from long-established usage, because of the fanciful conceit that from this finger a nerve went direct to the heart."

Frederick Saunders

SALAD FOR THE SOLITARY
AND THE SOCIAL
1871

And as this round
Is nowhere found
To flaw, or else to sever,
So let our love
As endless prove,
And pure as gold for ever.

Robert Herrick

The following are inscriptions taken from seventeenth- and eighteenth-century wedding rings:

This ring is a token I gave to thee,
That thou no tokens do change for me.

If in thy love thou constant bee,
My heart shall never part from thee.

The eye did find, ye heart did chuse,
The hand doth bind, till death doth loose.

Breake not thy vow to please the eye,
But keepe thy love, so live and dye.

Love him who gave thee this ring of gold,
'Tis he you must kiss thee when thou'rt old.

This circle, though but small about,
The devil, jealousie, shall keep out.

You and I will lovers be.

Thy consent is my content.

Of all the rest I love thee best.

THE CELEBRATION

The Bells

Hear the mellow wedding bells,—
Golden bells!
What a world of happiness their harmony
    foretells!
Through the balmy air of night
How they ring out their delight!
From the molten golden notes,
What a liquid ditty floats
To the turtle-dove that listens, while she
    gloats
On the moon!
Oh, from out the sounding cells,

What a gush of euphony voluminously wells!
How it swells!
How it dwells
On the Future! How it tells
Of the rapture that impels
To the swinging and the ringing
Of the bells, bells, bells,
Of the bells, bells, bells, bells,
Bells, bells, bells,—
To the rhyming and the chiming of the bells!

Edgar Allan Poe

Rice, a symbol of fertility, has been thrown at weddings since ancient times.

In old England, wedding guests would shower young newlyweds with nuts, shells, and even pieces of sod.

Wedding Cake

The tradition of the wedding cake dates to ancient Rome, where brides and grooms were presented with wheat and barley biscuits, which were later broken and sprinkled over the bride's head. The grains were a symbol of fertility, and crumbs were considered good-luck charms by the guests.

In the Middle Ages, wedding guests would bring sweet buns and stack them on a table at the wedding feast. After the ceremony, the bride and groom would kiss over the pile of cakes, in hopes of ensuring a long, happy life together.

Wedding cake has been believed to hold certain magic powers. "Cousin Debby was married a little while ago, and she sent me a piece of Bride-Cake to put under my pillow; and I had the sweetest dream—I thought we were going to be married together."

From a letter reprinted in
CONNOISSEUR,
February 20, 1775

"*Slices of the bridecake are put through the wedding ring: they are afterwards laid under pillows, at night, to cause young persons to dream of their lovers . . .*"

John Brand

OBSERVATIONS ON POPULAR ANTIQUES

1777

Traditional wedding cakes were made with fruits, nuts, and soaked with brandy or other liquor. The brandy preserved the cake, and the top tier would be saved and eaten upon the christening of the couple's first child.

Some Other Wedding Traditions

The tossing of the bouquet and the decking of the bridal car with cans and ribbons have a common origin.

Amongst the Greeks, Romans, and German peoples, it was a custom for the bride to remove her shoe and throw it to her guests as a symbol of good luck. Whoever caught the shoe would be the next to wed.

After the wedding feast, old shoes would be tied to the rear of the carriage taking the couple away. Shoes were symbolic of the exchange of property between the bride and groom.

Today, the bouquet is tossed by the bride, and cans and ribbons are used to decorate the car. In England, shoes are still tied to the bridal car.

In the Middle Ages, it was customary to remove the garters from both the bride and groom for luck. This event would take place inside the chapel after the wedding.

Beginning in the sixteenth century, this act would take place at the wedding feast—or within the bridal chamber itself.

"When Bed-time is come, the Bride-men pull of the Bride's Garters, which she had before unty'd, that they might hang down, and so prevent a curious Hand coming too near her Knee. This done, and the Garters being fasten'd to the Hats of the Gallants, the Bride-maids carry the Bride into the Bride-chamber, where they undress her, and lay her in Bed . . ."

Henry Mission

MEMOIRES ET OBSERVATIONS

1698

The text of this book was set in Nuptial Script by Berryville Graphics Digital Composition of Berryville, Virginia

Design by Maura Fadden Rosenthal

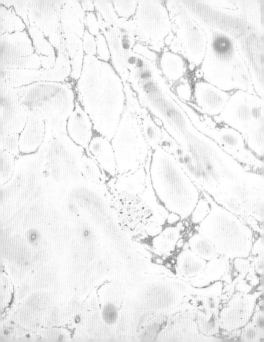